# Ninety/Ten (90/10) Rule of Money

## (A Brief Thoughts on Building a Profitable Business)

### By Celeste Young

# Contents

# Introduction

Getting your business profitable and cash positive is easier than you might think.

In fact, it can happen right now by reading this book.

I call it the 90/10 rule.

It's one of my favourite profit coaching tips that I share with my clients.

It's deceptively simple, works like a charm and can be implemented within the month.

If this is your first book on investment, and concerned that it might be too complicated, please do not be concerned. All I ask is to open up your mind and read this book from the beginning to the end.

In fact, by reading the entire book, you will know a lot more about investing than many people who are being paid to give their investment advice. In many ways, this book starts simple and remains simple.

# The Rule of Money (90/10)

I really appreciated the Italian economist Vilfredo Pareto's discovery of the 80/20 rule, also known as the Principle of Least Effort. Yet I was more aware of the 90/10 rule, which says that 10 percent of the people make 90 percent of the money.

Here's the concept. You're only allowed to operate on 90% of your company's monthly income. The other 10% is set aside in a separate account for taxes, extra debt payments and working capital. Simple, I know, but it rarely happens. Too many businesses operate on their full billings. If you've ever found yourself struggling to make payroll, you can relate to this.

I am concerned because more and more families are counting on their investments to support them in the future. The problem is that while more people are investing, very few of them are well-educated investors. What will happen to these new investors when the market crashes? The federal government of the United States insures the savings from catastrophic loss, but our investments are not insured. A wise man once asked to his mentor, "What advice would you give the average investor?" his reply was, "DON'T BE AVERAGE."

# How to Apply the 90/10 Rule

Start by grabbing a piece of paper. Write at the top of that paper what your company bills on average each month. You probably have some months that are better than others. That's fine. For now, give me a good average.

Let's pretend that your company bills $100,000 a month in revenue.

From that, take out 10%. You don't get to use that money. It's for taxes, paying off debt and saving for a rainy day. In this case, that would be $10,000.

This means that you have $90,000 left to make operational decisions on. You have to figure out how to pay for the following with that budget:

- Your entire wage for the month
- Marketing expenses (I suggest you spend 6 - 8% of revenues on marketing by the way)
- The cost of your materials and supplies
- All other overheard expenses
- Minimum debt payments
- All partner payments
- Any other balance sheet payments or monthly expenses

# Create a Plan

Sit down with your accountant and create a plan for how the 90% will be spent. Here's an example of how you might do that:

## $90,000 Budget

-$30,000 for labor

-$25,000 for materials and supplies

-$10,000 for your month's wage

-$8,000 for marketing

-$9,000 for partner payouts

-$5,500 for overhead

-$2,500 for minimum debt payments

The numbers will be specific to your business of course, but you get the idea. This doesn't have to be complicated.

I can't stand how difficult some accountants make this stuff. They'll create pages and pages of of Excel documents that link to each other in a myriad of ways. At the end of its creation, the only person that can use it is the accountant.

## The Only Exceptions to the 10 Percent

If you keep it simple, everyone can understand it and make better decisions.

## Can you Do More Than 10 Percent?

Some of you will already be beating the 90/10 rule and that's great! You're in the upper echelon of business and should pat yourself on the back.

The goal here is to constantly try to improve this ratio. Once you get to 90/10, shoot for 85/15 and so on. Wherever you're at, set a goal to make it better.

# What to Do With The 10 Percent?

Keep it in your savings account and forget about it. This will do several things for you:

1. It will create a buffer for when the economy decides to tank again, and it will.

2. It creates a nice cash balance to pay for your taxes if you end up owing at the end of the year.

3. It gives you options to grow. For example, if a recession hit, you could acquire competitors for pennies on the dollar. While everyone else is running for cover, you could be reigning supreme.

If you have debt, I want you to pay that off as quickly as possible. I don't care what anyone says. Some finance guys will argue that having debt is a good thing due to the time value of money, blah blah blah. I don't care. A business that is debt free will win every time. Mark my words.

In the budget example above, there was $2,500 set aside for minimum payments on debt. Your 10% can be used to pay extra towards the balance until you're out of debt. Once you've done that, the rest goes into savings. Period.

## Does It Ever Stop?

If I had my way, you would keep adding 10% or more to savings every month. At the very least, don't stop until you have 3 months of expenses built up in there. In our current example, the business is gobbling up $90,000 of cash every month. That would mean that once you hit $270,000 in savings, you can consider stopping. But I wouldn't if I were you.

## If You're Overspending

It's time to make some hard decisions if your business is spending more than 90%. It usually starts with looking at payroll.

Most companies have too many people on staff. I hate to be the guy that says you need to let people go, but be honest with yourself. Do you have people on your team that are not pulling their weight? Have you hired family members that you're terrified to let go? (Never hire family by the way).

The point is that if I were profit coaching you and your company, we would start here.

Once you have your team set up, we would then look at optimizing your relationships with suppliers so that you're not paying too much for your materials and supplies. This can take a bit longer, but it's always worth your time.

# What If You Are Not Spending 6-8 Percent on Marketing

My guess is that you're not. I rarely find a business that is. Most companies would cut their marketing budgets before they would let go of dead weight staff. The fear of confrontation is too great.

This is backwards. I'm always miffed when I see it.

If I were to guess, you're probably spending 1 - 2 % on marketing or less. If that's the case, I would suggest rearranging your budget so that you're investing in customer acquisition. Once you get that in line, figure out where to make cuts in payroll, etc. so that everything fits in that 90% or better range.

# Conclusion

Thank you for reading this short book. It's not hard. Anyone can do this. You're smart. I know, because you've started a business and have gotten as far as you have.

If all of this seems overwhelming, take a deep breath and focus on what matters. In the end, you'll have a business that's profitable and strong. Focus on how great that will feel, and nothing will stop you.

If this book helped you in any way, I'd like to ask you for a favour to be kind and leave a review for this book on Amazon.com.

Thanks,

**Celeste Young**

Make-up Guide, Make-up Looks, Beauty Styles and Looks, Inner Beauty, Marriage, Beauty with Heart

http://www.amazon.com/CELESTES-BEAUTY-INSIDE-AND-OUT-ebook/dp/B01AX9KLDI

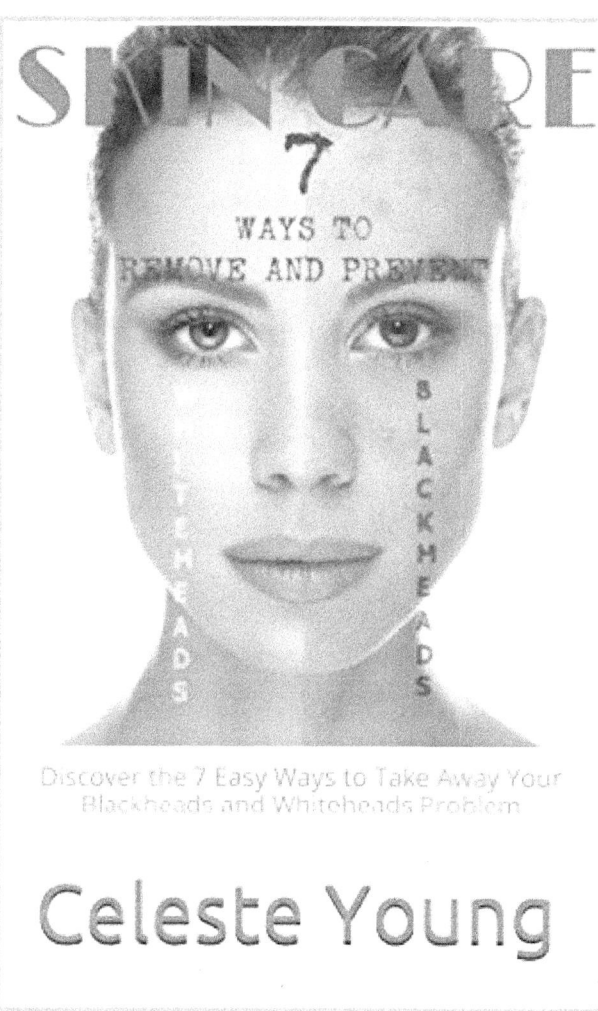

SKINCARE

7

WAYS TO
REMOVE AND PREVENT

WHITEHEADS

BLACKHEADS

Discover the 7 Easy Ways to Take Away Your
Blackheads and Whiteheads Problem

## Celeste Young

SEX POSITIONS

13 Ultimate Sex Positions [Chinese New Year Edition], Discover the Number 1 and Most Pleasurable Sex Position that Wanted by All

CELESTE YOUNG

amazon.com/author/lynnel.anne

AUTHOR PAGE

# Conclusion

Thank you for reading this short book. It's not hard. Anyone can do this. You're smart. I know, because you've started a business and have gotten as far as you have.

If all of this seems overwhelming, take a deep breath and focus on what matters. In the end, you'll have a business that's profitable and strong. Focus on how great that will feel, and nothing will stop you.

If this book helped you in any way, I'd like to ask you for a favour to be kind and leave a review for this book on Amazon.com.

Thanks,

**Celeste Young**